Quelle Histoire

Publishing and design: Unique Heritage Editions SAS, 141, boulevard Ney, 75018 Paris
Illustrations: Bruno Wennagel, Mathieu Ferret, Mathilde Tuffin, Guillaume Biasse, Nuno Alves Rodrigues, Camille Mertz, Marianne Tesseraud
Text: Patricia Crété
Editor: Leslie-Fleur Picardat
Artistic direction / Layout: Kayna Toung

Registered office: 141, boulevard Ney 75018 Paris

www.quellehistoire.com

Printed in Romania by Rotolito

Legal deposit May 2024

Law n°49-956 of 16 July 1949 on publications for young persons

LITTLE WHYS

6 JUNE 1944

The Normandy Landings

In this book you'll discover everything that happened before, during and after the Normandy landings, which took place on 6 June 1944. Who organised this operation? Why was this location chosen? Which troops participated? What weapons were used? As you turn the pages you'll experience this great event of the Second World War alongside American paratroopers, British commando frogmen, Canadian troops and the French 'Commando Kieffer'.

HOW DID THE IDEA OF A LANDING ARISE?

It all started in September 1939 at the outbreak of the Second World War. France and a large part of Europe were very quickly invaded and then occupied by Nazi Germany, which implemented a terrible policy on the population. This called for urgent action! So, in September 1941, a meeting took place in Moscow between the USSR, the United States and the United Kingdom, who formed an alliance against the enemy. By 1942, these three powers were planning to mount a huge military operation: the Soviets were already fighting in Eastern Europe, so the Allies had to open a new front in the West to trap the German forces in a pincer movement. This is how the idea of a landing arose!

WHAT WAS OPERATION OVERLORD?

Plans for the offensive gradually took shape. It was given a codename: Operation Overlord! The plan was simple... The first phase of the operation involved landing Allied troops and equipment on the beaches of Normandy, France, and then securing the area. The second phase was to advance the troops and liberate the cities occupied by the German enemy. As you can imagine, this was a massive operation!

WHY DO MILITARY OPERATIONS HAVE CODENAMES?

As you may have guessed, military operations must remain top secret. Codenames are therefore used to prevent the enemy from discovering the locations of the battles! The codename chosen for this offensive was 'Overlord'. Other missions during the Second World War had equally strange names such as Neptune, Jubilee, Fortitude, etc.

WHY WAS NORMANDY CHOSEN FOR THE LANDINGS?

It was at the Tehran Conference, held from 28 November to 1 December 1943, that American President Franklin Roosevelt, Soviet leader Joseph Stalin and British Prime Minister Winston Churchill decided on the location of the landings: Normandy, France. But why here? Because the Normandy beaches were large enough to accommodate thousands of troops, tanks and supplies. They were also less well defended than the beaches in Pas-de-Calais or Belgium.

HOW MANY BEACHES WERE INVOLVED?

Five Normandy beaches were selected, and each was assigned a codename: Utah, Omaha, Gold, Juno and Sword. All would witness the landing of Allied soldiers, who were assigned to a beach based on their nationality: the Americans disembarked on Utah and Omaha; the British on Gold, Juno (with the Canadians) and Sword (with the French).

WHO LED OPERATION OVERLORD?

American General Dwight Eisenhower was selected to command SHAEF; the Supreme Headquarters of the Allied Expeditionary Forces. Once he took office in January 1944, he assembled his team and brought in General Montgomery. Together, they planned the landings. They were the masterminds and strategists behind the operation!

WHAT COASTAL DEFENCES HAD THE GERMANS PUT IN PLACE?

The Germans had feared an Allied landing for some time, and in August 1942 Adolf Hitler, the leader of Nazi Germany, tasked General Rommel with constructing the Atlantic Wall. This was an extensive system of coastal defences built along the west coast of Europe from northern Norway to the Spanish border. It comprised a series of blockhouses, buried shelters and fortifications. The beaches were mined and rigged with stakes, traps and barriers. However, by 1944, construction was far from complete, which proved a huge advantage for the Allies and their landing operation!

HOW WAS THE DATE CHOSEN?

Operation Overlord was initially planned for May 1944. However, for the operation to be carried out in the best possible conditions, a number of meteorological factors had to be met: good weather, plenty of moonlight to facilitate night-time operations and a tide high enough to disembark the soldiers and tanks.

However, the date was postponed due to persistent bad weather, combined with a lack of equipment (notably barges). General Eisenhower then set the date for 5 June, but a storm rolled in, so it was postponed until the next day, 6 June! Once launched, the operation lasted until late August 1944.

WHAT PLOYS DID THE ALLIES USE TO DECEIVE THE ENEMY?

The Allied command had a brainwave: to fool the enemy into thinking that the landing would take place elsewhere, in Norway or Pas-de-Calais. A military deception strategy called 'Fortitude' was then devised by an intelligence expert. In the south of England, the Allies assembled tanks made of rubber, artillery pieces made of plastic and fake wooden ships, built by film set designers. They then made false announcements on the radio and appointed the American General George Patton to lead a fictitious general staff. And it worked: the Germans were left in a state of confusion!

WHAT WAS THE ALLIES' PLAN OF ATTACK ON D-DAY?

D-Day finally arrived, and Operation Overlord was launched during the night of 5 to 6 June! As ships full of soldiers headed out to sea, various measures were taken to ensure they could disembark safely. At around midnight, paratroopers were dropped beyond the beaches to secure the area.

From 3:00 am, planes started flying over the German positions and launched an aerial bombardment. From 5:30 am, warships took over and bombarded the enemy blockhouses. Finally, the first barges landed at approx. 6:30 am and the troops disembarked to start the assault on the beaches.

WHICH FORCES WERE DEPLOYED BY THE ALLIES ON THAT DAY?

In total, almost 156,000 men landed on the five Normandy beaches on 6 June: 133,000 by sea and 23,000 by air. To cross the English Channel, they used 4,266 transport ships, escorted by 722 warships. 11,500 bombers, fighters and gliders criss-crossed the skies to protect them.

WHAT WEAPONS WERE USED?

The majority of the troops, whatever their nationality, were equipped with a rifle and grenades for their assault on the beaches. They were supported by tanks, some of which were mine-resistant, ditch-filling, flame-throwing or amphibious (with a 'skirt' that enabled them to float); these specialist tanks were known as 'Funnies'. What a cool name!

WHAT ROLE DID THE PARATROOPERS PLAY?

On 6 June, the clock had barely struck midnight before the paratroopers were in action. British paratroopers were dropped near the Orne, the river that flows into the English Channel close to the landing beaches. Their mission was to take control of the bridges and destroy any German defences that could prevent the soldiers from reaching the hinterland. The American paratroopers were dropped behind Utah Beach to secure the surrounding villages, however many of them fell into waterlogged marshes. Despite heavy losses on both sides, the missions were a success.

WHAT HAPPENED ON UTAH BEACH?

The first barges docked on Utah Beach at 6:30 am. Hundreds of men gradually spilled out onto the sand, followed by 28 amphibious tanks. It was only then that they realised they had drifted more than 2 km away from the area initially planned, having been carried by strong currents. But no matter...They had to press on! It was low tide, and the enemy traps were clearly visible. The soldiers wasted no time in destroying them while trying to avoid the fire from the German batteries. Utah Beach was secured at approximately 8:00 am; the men were ready for action and the various war vehicles left the beach.

AND ON OMAHA BEACH?

At 6:30 am, the first wave of American troops landed on Omaha Beach, followed by the second wave. And that was when all hell broke loose... The nighttime bombardments had missed their target, and the German defence system was intact. Dozens of men were killed, barges burst into flame and many tanks were sunk. It was not until around 10:00 am that battleships arrived off the coast to bombard the enemy positions. A few men took advantage of the situation to climb the embankments and catch the Germans by surprise. Meanwhile, others cleared mines from the beach. The losses were considerable, but by the end of the day the Allies had regained control of Omaha!

AND ON GOLD BEACH?

British troops set foot on Gold Beach at 7:25 am. To evacuate the beach as quickly as possible, they relied on their Funnies and Crab tanks, which detonated mines and created safe routes. This enabled the soldiers to slip through the gaps in the German defences and head inland. This beach was crucial, as the Allies had planned to assemble floating jetties on it which, once connected, would serve as a deep-water port, known as 'Port Winston'. It was installed in just a few days and transported nearly 10,000 tons of equipment and several thousand men daily. Amazing!

AND ON JUNO BEACH?

As on Gold Beach, the British, with the support of the Canadian troops, sprang into action. Just before the landings, frogmen moved the German defence systems under the sea, which was a good idea! However, the weather conditions still managed to throw a spanner in the works, and some barges hit rocks in the heavy swell and quickly sank. The amphibious tanks, the Duplex Drives, struggled to keep afloat in the waves. Casualties were high, but the German defences were finally crushed by the British tanks, while the Canadian forces took control of the beach.

AND ON SWORD BEACH?

Further to the east, Sword Beach was the last beach involved in the operation. The Funnies tanks landed there at 7:25 am, followed shortly by the British troops. It was then the turn of the 177 men of the Commando Kieffer, who were recognisable by their famous green berets; they were the only French troops present on 6 June 1944. The German lines of defence had already been breached, and the Allied soldiers stormed inland while the beach was cleared of traps by the most experienced soldiers. By the end of the day, the area had been secured!

WHY IS LORD LOVAT FAMOUS?

Some of the soldiers who landed became famous; for example, the Scottish general Simon Fraser, better known as Lord Lovat, who arrived on Sword Beach. But he was not alone! At his side was his faithful piper, Bill Millin, who played as loudly as he could, and who went on to accompany his general at all the battlefields of Normandy!

WHICH COUNTRIES TOOK PART IN THE LANDINGS?

The nationalities of the troops who landed on 6 June were American, Canadian and British, not forgetting the 177 French members of the Commando Kieffer. But that's not all: they were supported by contingents from France, Belgium, Luxembourg, the Netherlands, Norway, Denmark, Poland, Czechoslovakia, Greece, Australia, New Zealand and South Africa. No fewer than 15 nations were represented on that day!

DID ANY NATIVE AMERICANS TAKE PART IN THE LANDINGS?

Yes, many Native Americans enlisted. Charles Shay, a young Penobscot, was one of the medic soldiers who landed on Omaha Beach. Comanches also helped to throw the Germans off the scent: using their language, which only they understood, they transmitted information over the radio about operations in progress, meaning that the Germans never managed to decipher it!

AND WHAT DID THE LOCALS DO?

Some locals, the resistance fighters, prepared the ground, while others acted as the circumstances dictated, like Geneviève Duboscq, who lived in Sainte-Mère-Église, near Utah Beach. She was only 12 years old at the time but ventured out in the middle of the night with her parents to rescue 350 American paratroopers who had fallen in flooded areas. They were awarded the US Guard of Honor medal in recognition of their vital assistance.

WHAT WAS THE HUMAN TOLL OF OPERATION OVERLORD?

On the evening of 6 June, it was time to take stock... On the Allied side, around 10,500 of the 156,000 troops that had landed that day were dead, wounded, missing or taken prisoner. The beach that was hardest hit was Omaha, which accounted for 30% of the casualties. On the German side, almost 10,000 soldiers were killed or wounded. And what about the rest of the operation? 37,000 Allies were killed and 163,000 wounded, while on the German side, 80,000 were killed or missing, 170,000 were wounded and 200,000 were taken prisoner. But we mustn't forget the civilian victims (the locals): some historians estimate the death toll to be 20,000!

WHAT WAS THE OBJECTIVE AFTER THE LANDINGS?

Although the troops had endured the ordeal of D-Day, their mission was far from over! Initially, the aim was to liberate Normandy, but this was no easy task due to the Normandy '*bocages*': pastureland divided into small, hedged fields, which were difficult for the tanks to cross. Nonetheless, the Allies liberated almost 400 Normandy towns between 6 June and 12 September, the date Le Havre was taken. And there was more to come! The Allies then recaptured Paris, and this major advance enabled them to enter Berlin in April 1945 and defeat the German enemy.

HOW DO WE KNOW SO MUCH ABOUT THE NORMANDY LANDINGS?

On D-Day, no fewer than 17 war reporters were present on the beaches alongside the troops. The best known was Colin Wills, an Australian journalist, who spoke to the BBC that evening: "The whole sky is bright... the great battleships in the background are blazing away at the shore." The photographer Robert Capa followed the American troops on Omaha Beach and, risking his life, took 119 photos, some of which can still be seen to this day. Today, several museums and military cemeteries commemorate this key event in the Second World War, and you can visit them!

TO FIND OUT MORE

If you want to learn more about the Normandy landings, you can read books and visit museums and places of remembrance!

VISITS
Museums

There are various museums you can visit to gain a better understanding of the events of 6 June 1944. The oldest of these is the D-Day Museum in Arromanches, which opened on 5 June 1954. You can also visit the Caen Memorial, the Overlord Museum near Omaha Beach, or the Utah Beach Landing Museum. Not forgetting the Grand Bunker at Ouistreham, a museum dedicated to the Atlantic Wall.

VISITS
Cemeteries

You can also pay your respects at the military cemeteries, which pay tribute to the fallen soldiers. One of the best known is the American cemetery at Colleville-sur-Mer, next to Omaha beach. But don't forget the British cemetery at Bayeux, with its 4,648 white graves, and the German cemetery at La Cambe, with its 2,122 black graves (in accordance with German tradition).

VISITS

Experience it for yourself!

The Normandy Victory Museum in Carentan invites families to take a flight on a transport aircraft, the C-47. You can also discover military vehicles and even climb aboard a barge. At the Airborne Museum in Sainte-Mère-Église, you can find out what happened to the paratroopers who dropped over the town: you'll hear the planes revving their engines and the exploding bombs… it's an impressive experience.

BOOKS

Children: the heroes!

You can also learn so much from the comfort of your own home… Why not read the novel written by Geneviève Duboscq: *My Longest Night – A twelve-year-old heroine's stirring account of D-Day and after* (French title: *Dans la nuit du Débarquement*), which tells the story of how, aged just 12 years old, she helped rescue American paratroopers; or the book by Bertrand Solet: *The Shortest Night* (French title: *La Nuit la plus courte*), which describes how two children witnessed the Allied landings. Happy reading!

AND MORE

If you ask lots of questions about history and "just because" is never enough of an answer, this book is for you!

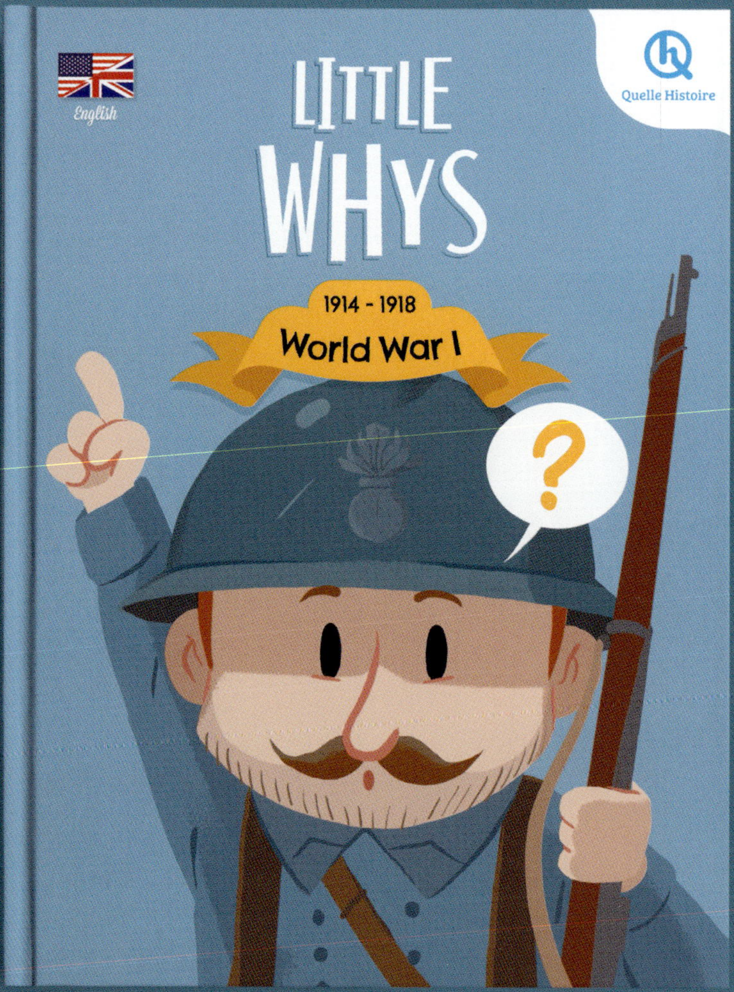